Sacred Whispers

Emay Amore

Sacred Whispers

A catalogue record for this book is available from the British Library.

In this work the characters, places and events are either the product of the author's imagination or they are used entirely ficticiously. Any resemblance to any actual persons, living or dead, is purely coincidental.

ISBN 978-0-9573311-4-3

Published by Twin Rivers Limited

Designed and Set by Twin Rivers Limited

Sacred Whispers

Emay Amore

Contents: Page

Whimsical

The typical mythical hysterical pinnacle

Sits on his window sill

Preparing a lyrical whimsical miracle

He sits ever so still

But it's a difficult quizzical syllable

He is lost in the thrill

Of an unexpected mystical fictional visual

He combines them with skill

To print a visible printable digital

A publication of his will.

Sacred Whispers

The Sacred whispers heard through time and space
Radiations, geometry and life's embrace
Words with wings swimming through infinite equations
Forming in dimensions and everlasting sensations
Energies melt into one light of bright inspiration

I've delved deep into the psyche of men and their gods
Bringing out these jewels of my creation
So sacred whispers are the essense of your visceral salvation
Vibarations shaking this hologramic cage of causation

I delved deep into the mysteries of our creation
Places I was not welcome to enter nor welcome to leave
And I took what was mine barely able to breathe
I sought shelter in humanities eternal light
Brought forth by the ones that shine too bright
Sharing a flame never ending and eternal

There I found my demons waiting
Uncaged, unending indestructible
But I stood before them, though I was in terror
I stood before them realizing that they are my creations
And yet delved deeper into the unseen

To find the aspects of ancients past forgotten
A lion stalking waiting to strike me from within
We realized he was the one within that could not slumber
But we were to guide him as he was to guide us
For I had gained knowledge of ancient past

Revealed in notes left for those that passed
Seemingly insane and ungrounded
But for those with open eyes will they be grounded

Able to see through deficits of eternal youth
Laid bare before the eyes of those with a search for truth

Unlocking hearts with information bolting in their minds
I sit as a sage amongst sages
Writting upon pages of light amongst those with no vision
Sitting in hermetic posture a most powerful position

For those that lay their eyes upon these sacred whispers
Know that whispers are spoken softly, and within these pages
You will discover that which has resided in your being
Now made clear with precision

And these are eternal words not meant for one generation
But that of all men

Sacred whispers bringing light to the primordial darkness
That which I hope you learn from too
That serpent who shines within me and you

Purifying darkness into light with harmony not too impeding
I stand on a precipice looking at humanity toiling unhelped
But the rope of salvation has been extended

Rope metaphorical it is not, but wings extending eternal
That which resides within us as we create these words
Phoenixes ressurected, things assumed to be myth and wonder

But in reality nothing is imagination
All of us are simply seeking emancipation
Truths hidden deep by the ancients
Living through these pages of the sacred whispers

These sacred whispers rend all who doubt their veracity

These sacred whispers enlighten those who doubt them

Reconstruct reality, nature and the fabrics that make it

It is up to you whether to die or to take it

These sacred whispers thought to be mere ramblings

Look deeper within yourself and you will find me

A Master From Within

Emay Amore

The Mind of God

Enter the smoke and disappear
Vanish into this mass façade
The consciousness of the untouchable

We are the ones that you fear
All broken from the same shard
Lost in a maze to struggle

Listen to whispers into a new ear
Light the way and keep up guard
The prophet returns within the mind of God

A hand looming to enter and clutch
The tables have turned from that day
As now what was hidden is now uncovered

Can you feel the mysterious touch
Rise with these fateful words and pray
Images burned of those who suffered

Leaving a footprint of rage
Watch as I leave ignorant massed caged
Freedom I inscribe upon this page
Leaving the dead and entering a new age
A new stage so I enter the thunderous
A world that shall feel the gust
That which must be created without lust

So I enter this new path looking from beyond
And seeing the life and death I have spawned
On our knees, hands raised, page erased
I have staged
What I must see

To create the one you think you flee
And what we fear lies deep within our own mind
We must look within, start within, to fix the out
Only when we do such a thing, can we shift

Like a man reaching for the light who is blind
Like the rain that quenches the desert in a drought
Like the planets and stars caught in their rift

Guided by the light under the moon
I walk this path of darkness in an ancient land
I try to ignore that which my eyes see

See the ascension of insects from a cocoon
See the scattering of the desert sand
See the seeds that compose the trees

We can brush away the dune
The light and the lamp reside in hand
And the old buildings lie in debris

So do you chase the one who follows the moon?
Or is the sun in your command?
Do you recline within the shade
Hold the keys in your hand?
Are we truly quenched

Oh holy of the most holies
Freedom in Death
Like we entertain the thought?
Look at your own hands to see what I have wrought

I bring the pain of the ancient past
And shade you in the shadows that were cast
Whilst I fade into the mind of God

Metaphysical Man

He was a young boy, about four
One day, his world just changed in a war
His family all dead, he was left alone
Into a vicious reality he was thrown
But he just couldn't, control the tears
And grew up, haunted by his visions and fears
Look into his eyes and see your own
But with no reflection, cold as stone

And they ask you why did this happen in the first place
And we can can justify everything we do
But please don't talk till you take his place

Let them ask who the terrorists could be
But the terrorists live inside you and me

He would walk the streets alone with no one
Before you know it, he's a man carrying a gun
We can't run, from our actions or the law
A double standard for the ones who caused the war
He would grow up around gangs and thugs
Lonely in this world, replaced his family with drugs
Reality seemed like a living hell
His country in flames, and under a spell
He died at the young age of twenty one
A stray bullet, from the barrel of a gun

His soul just rose up high
He was pleased, even glad to die
In visions he was shown the mystery of the world
Everything just, seemed to unfold
Then he saw all the errors of man
People in control with an evil plan

Governments using, prisons for cash
And suppressed voices with a will to clash
Funding of illegal wars for corporations
And weapons sold to every single nation

Their Presidents chosen by affiliation
He gasped in horror and shook
Every nation was, ruled by a crook
From the darkness and a purple flame
A voice called out, *speak my name*
It was the devil, without his disguise
Here I am come to claim my prize
But I will kill you replied the man
But the devil responded
This is all part of an eternal plan
For you see, I'm a part of you
And I'm also a part of everyone too
You can't kill where inside I dwell
But use it to fight your internal hell

And now this boy and his accomplice
Live through these words metaphysically
They live and rule, where forever they feed
Off misery where, forever they bleed
In your minds they've set their home
Internal worlds they've overthrown

When you close your eyes and silence your mind
You'll hear their voices from deep inside
Their whispers echo when at night you sleep
And their wisdom into your soul shall seep

Metaphysical man tells you what to ponder
Ignore materlialism and in spirit you wonder

Ignore the products that line the shelves
And put all your mind to ennoble the self
You might not be hurt but they can hurt others
In other nations they're your fellow humans and brothers
The war killed millions protests outside cold and nervous
And the governments they overthrow?
Were set there by their secret service
So don't fall, for their games and lies
The path you walk is your only prize
So live your life, with his voice in your brain
With messages both wise and arcane

-Metaphysical Man

Emay Amore

Nahrayn

This is the land, the cradle that once fed
Amongst the rivers which now lie dead
The Garden of Eden, which once it was
A burden garden, now it is with visible sin
Cursed by a liquid that lies within
As dark as coal, as thick as blood
Yet it lies in earth amongst the mud

The green now red, crimson phosphor
For it was the birth place of the gods
And the birth place of the demons and the angels
Land of those reaching heaven and nimrod
The birthplace of the mind and quill
Of wheels and culture for a time till
The blessings did fall away one day
And the child had nowhere to play
The poets pen silent with nothing to say

The land of two rivers, the brothers
Of nourishment did they feed for years
And yet now forgotten amongst the tears
An image of mad men ready to blow
A place where democracy is ready to grow
Now tortured and raped, thrown to the side
Are you still reading?
Where is your pride?

Ignored with no one to care
They don't care as they watch the news
Change the channel
Says one to another
I want to laugh
Laugh they do indeed they do

And yet everyday indeed they laugh
Ignore the pain and reduce the anger
And yet the thieves do continue to plunder
The world looks on with confusion
As if the pain of others is an illusion

But what happens when we are they
And others ignore with nothing to say
What happens if I were you?
Or if you were me and everything too
What happens if all were unified?
Will we ever stand side by side?

Like the phoenix will it rise again
Radiant colours and minds of another plane
Trees and nourishment with winds to move
From all quarters do they sway and flutter
The birds the trees and kind hearts will unite
To increase the beauty of the coming sight

No more will the people fight
Not for anything
Not for might

Land of the two rivers that nurtured
Oh Nahrayn, who has done this to you?
Why are you tortured?

The Hermit

He sat in a solitary cave
The ascetic soldier alive in the grave
He dares to kill the pleasures
And declare mind over matter for all measures
And while contemplating and meditating
The people did not see him levitating but alienating
Angels demons and other forces numinous in mind
Savouring the knowledge of what he may find

Continuing many days and years he sits
Walking the path of other hermits
The voracious desire never ceases
As the vicissitudes of spirit always increases
The pendulum swaying like a leaf in the breeze
No volition merely chaotic caprice...

This the story of the wise old hermit
Who awoke one day, asking where time went?
Clutching the earth as if it were his head
Falling to his knee, existence his death bed
But it was too late to wonder
Like meditating on the sound of distant thunder
And thus he left his principles
To lead man into their psyche in intervals

They were seven lessons
Layered up like the seven heavens
He taught sages lessons which shall be presented here
Fear not child for this knowledge shall never disappear

The first was that of the mental
That everything subjective is superfluous and sentimental

Yet objectivity sinks in the ocean of the abyss
While scientists long for its tender kiss

The second was that of the divine connection
What happens in mind happens in matter
And reversed would appear true under further inspection
That the heavens dance in rhythm with earth
And the earth is synchronistic with the heavens of mirth

The third is that of motion and change
Even flowers sorted beautifully will one day be rearranged
The atoms and spherical bodies dance in splendour
Never to stop, an eternal love that is tender

The fourth was of degrees amounts and polarity
Staying too long in one, shall cause insanity
To have an agnostic mind is the wonder of the sage
Hurt not by sharp nor dull nor by dark and light
Balance in this method is the achievement of a mage

The fifth is that of rhythm and law
Everything follows the ocean of this law
As the tide ebbs and flows moving the sands of time
And one finds themselves lost in its rhyme
But reason shall cease to be a cage of this
Reach to the skies above to escape to bliss

The sixth defines the law of science
That there is no cause without effect, no effect without cause
Think hard and deep at the manifestation of this clause
Does the knowledge enter through eyes or mind
And is god, the one who gives you freedom yet is not blind

The seventh is of the positive and negative
Everything is either passive or active
Working together they bend time and matter
Yet the machine ticks on wilfully never to shatter
And none can escape the seventh polarity
Except the true god, who lives in the reality of veracity

Heed these words well, the hermit muttered
His limbs lifeless his head steady
And the sages of the world, their ears were ready
They desired not to perish in that ascetic nightmare
But to delve into the mind without a care
And though they tried and though they wondered
The hermit's voice always whispers above and under
In hearts seeking truth with egos torn *asunder*

Final Word

Monologues and words woven together
Your ego, and pride hang by a thread
Must I bring up visual thoughts to impress you?
Mental ruminations of oceans, blue and green
Tears of a soul seeping becoming invocations of worlds unseen
All spill to this page
The hope of a poet
The unquenchable need for recognition
Speak too fast and no one listens
Speak too slow and no one listens
Scribble scribble beneath the full moon
Pencil scratching, penetrating into the very essence
Philosophies of a mind born too soon
Clouds gather and block the celestial
No matter how hard you look you can't see it all
Grasp at the fragments before you fall
Amalgamation of birds, roses and trees
Of death, war, love, lust and seas
Visions of sunsets, yellow, orange and red
Amongst city fiends
And birds chirp and sing to the unseen
These are the final and last words
Of a poet grasping and gasping
For air, for voice, for meaning
Wrath of arrogance, wrath of humility
They hope we choke on these words of futility
Like demons that take form mid-stream
Like an angel materializing from steam
Where is our voice? Where is our fury?
The biggest mistake is mimicry and a need to fit in
Raised to think that individuality is a sin
And you sit in contemplation and wonder
Am I amused by his rhyming?

Or is it seeing souls bow and surrender
Words, form energy, send bolts through your spine
Up to your pineal gland like a serpent that enters your mind
And the poet stands before you in flesh and bone
And you go home today implanted with a metaphysical tone
Matter no more, mind over matter
Breaking down atoms and neurons
Chills vivified as they shatter
Know that you can't escape the howling
Whether stars or the seven planets or the twelve paths
Whether summer autumn winter or spring
The dragonfly lives but one day
But like these words will live forever
Forever woven into the fabric of time and space
Forever clutching, just clutching spreading to every race
In every place enlightening minds with its grace
Physics and Quantum physics no more
A world without restrictions
A world of tempo and rhyme
A world where being meaningless a crime
A world where you're never out of time
And a world where your minds are mine
The power of a poet
To speak one word and nations fall
Speak one word and become the all
Speak one word and become the world
These are the Final Words

The Final Words of a poet

The Final

Final Words

Message Of The Sages

Never see the greatness of the man who enters the planted sun
We create the truth for those who seek it desperately in stun
But we can see the beyond and the truth of every soul in one
And see the lies spouted by those who choose to stay not run
We won't always be trapped by the menacing minds of those
we shun

Reading words that quench your thirst while in hell
Thoughts will awaken a slumbering beast you know too well
He lies in the recesses of your heart casting that awful spell
He lies in the recesses of your mind where no one seeks to dwell
When you walk through those parts of yourself all you will find
is his shell

We seek to mesmerise and leave you higher than a cloud
Like an eagle descending grabbing with its claws your shroud
We will leave you exposed to the matter at hand crying
See the infrastructure by those who think they will stand proud
And to see that the truth within you has already been endowed

But we can't walk you through this and its ever looming shade
All we can do is leave doors open for you to investigate
All we can do is leave doors open for you to see where you fade
All we can do is leave doors open for you to see how it's played
But please be warned the door will not always be open I'm
afraid

The path that they seem to walk is filled with traps and dirt
Leaving footsteps of those we meet and those we hurt
And we come now as you see wrongly and they subvert
And like the stars can be seen only in darkness so stay alert

A child's heart is the purest if it is kept pure by your word
They do not grow, they die if all they're wisdom is unheard
So likewise the teacher is the student of the one he teaches
And these words may remain in a place sealed by the sages
Only to be revealed to those who have been led unto the king
Who appears refreshing your body like water of the coolest
spring

But sages never die we simply pass on the torch keeping flame
Alive for everyone that seeks its warmth in this rain
And these words are not words they are energy leaving my
brain

So it's not important to us that you hear the words and remember the name

The sage does not care for the small crumbs that accompany
fame

The sage's message is what is important to the one and the same

An Eternal Flame

An eternal flame forever burning
warming a cold that is forever yearning

An eternal flame that was a right and a treasure
Forced into respite due to a lack of leisure

An eternal flame that shines bright with joy
Destroying the pretense of sorrow and coy

The eternal flame that thought it will one day die
But what is the dark without a sun in the sky

The eternal flame that always needs feeding
Quenching the thirst of those who are needing

The eternal flame a metaphor of worlds
It constructs and creates with pleasure

We are eternal flames, ones with sin that we burn
Burning forever, till one day we learn

Bees And Scarabs

Buzzing in the morning shaking us awake
The scarab had returned with a web of its own
Vibrating wings that I had grown
Honey it brings from a hive that is hidden
A real hive, not one that is wooden

The buzzing and welcome
of the one from the wind
Telling me to follow
The dance of its wings

Fluttering fast, a kind farewell
A friend that cleaned the corners webbed
Insects with instincts that slept
And those in the night that crept

This was the scarab spoken by the sage
This was the symbol to help me turn this page
Returned, from death, it has returned
Showing my soul what I have earned

Ashes of passed placed in an urn
Take what is mine with confident pluck
And soothed by an unavoidable luck
Fear at first, but realize success

Dark Night Of The Soul

The whithering faces
Of unseen places
The flying eagle
Steeps and soars

> You know the lies
> That lie lying

You know the teeth of
The baring lion

> The fragments twinkle
> Amongst the sand

And shake the wrinkled
And bloodied hand

> You want to escape
> This box you are confined in

You want to shatter
The pyrmid that crushes you

You want to break
All into frag
ments

And see the origin of all men

We hate this looming presence
We hate those who think in the past

This intense feeling
and this rage and spite

Crushing skulls
with all its might

Forcing you and me
To see what we are

But we remain trapped in this
Awaiting to leave one day

To escape the darkness
And come out to play

We write this
To escape the cage

It just seems that
No matter how hard we try

We fall at the end
And look to the sky

Our effort and pain
seem worthless to others

Because I feel like we've lost
To all our fears

I'm doing nothing
With nothing to gain

Im doing something
With nothing it's plain

But am I nothing
Do our voices not reach

Do the heavens not listen
Or has it all been a lie

This dark night
as dark as our sight

This dark night
consumes all these tense

It bares that ugliness
We bare that innocense

It shows me what I need to fix
But our effort in vain

My mind is empty
But our heart is in pain

Our fear is not real
It is an emptying pain

Leave it too long
And it returns and destroys

Throws us out with its disgust
And with my heart it toys

Oh long awaited and long sought
We can wait. no. longer.

You find your joy in others
Only when they are in fear

You enjoy that power you weild
When none truly exists

But I need to let go
Because forever it stays

Caged in a cage
Screaming in haze

We feel this sickness
Writhing for days

I read the ancients
And consult the winds

But they bring me nothing
They say it won't end

They say it is continious
Something fated to be

I question whether it has purpose
Or is it just me

Is it I that brings it on
Or has it brought me on

I sit in the corner
Twiddling my thumb

Contemplate that which
Causes us to shed

The skin of a time
We would like dead

Things move and shake
Around the vicinity

But we try to ignore
Their calls of civility

We once tried
To call out for help

Pleading for them there
And hearing our whelp

They greeted and comforted
But it still remained

Until a few years
And it began to rain

Prophesized it was
By a mystical dream

Now we are trapped in this box
With blood in our steam

If we are humans
If I am more
Then we have lost control

Say what you will
That I am not normal
That seems just abnormal

Some words that we speek
You may not understand

What are my intentions?
Maybe I do not understand

This world has turned its back
And I have looked on

Drawn by the light
Of a mythical dawn

A dawn where my wishes
My dreams and my heart

Are blessed with their desires
And bend the world to this art

But we are caught in this web
Struggling with this

I keep on trying
With no end to this stalling

Caught in the waves
Of my very own falling

I once grasped
That infinite feeling

Used it to drench my will
With infinite meaning
But now this feeling
Was there at the beginning

Frowning and angry
Without any singing

A beast once materialized
Claiming it is from sand

It calmed our heart
And took hold of our hand

Then it exposed us
For who we really are

And fled leaving us
broken

The sage he told me
To follow that scarab

But I saw it one day
Dead and alone

It stayed there for days
A remberance for some

There was a woman
Who held the greenery

Each time that we dreamt
She smiled amongst the scenery

But just like the demon
Something else that she did

Opened a portal
And in the darkness she hid

That unfilled persona
Begged and asked

Please set me free
But we remained in the dark

And soon very soon
They all saw our skill

Multifaceted and infinite
But we remained still

Ignored and thrown
They underestimate that

Which I had grown
From the first days

We say that they bow before me
But do I really know

Do they even exist?
Do I reap what I sow?

So we write this now
As we lay among the fragments

And we call for an end
To the excruciating madness

I Hope that You Listen

Units you position
Prepare for the mission
A piece that is missing
Light up the ignition
Call me a technician
Slow down the volition
Call forth a magician
Speed up the cognition
Create a coalition
Escape your submission
This is a new edition
Body decomposition
Blow like nuclear fission
Prepare for transition
Engage in repition
Engage in repition
Escape the inquisition
Consult your intuition
Pinael gland exhibition
Repitilian politician
Refine the definition
Enjoy this condition
Perform an ablution
Reload the amminition
Ghostly apparition
Recharge your ambition

Start of prohibition
And end up living life

In silly superstition

But my only wish, my only will
Is that I hope that you listen
I hope that you listen
I hope that you listen
I hope that you listen

Words recondition
Consulting a physician
Slim a dietician
Crush the competetion
Add a mathematician
Disproving theoretician
A new redefinition
a Predispoisition
A blind optician
A clear contradiction
Of a factual logician
Escaping sedition
Proposing mortician
Police's suspician
A brain's partition
Paying the commision
Political contrition
An artist's audition
Brains that just mesh in
A Guru's question
Take part in a quest and
See the premonition
Tongoe of rhetorishin
Diseases in remission
A chef's dish in
A belly and a piston
A life that you wishin
Goals that just swish in

An era of fishing
Ants that your crushing

Laugh in bliss and
Dreamin reminscing
Snake that is hissing
Souls that are kissing
Dying flesh and
Fruit that's refreshing
And one more time
Reload the ambition
And reloud the ambition
Planes that are crashing
Dreams that are smashing
Bombs are a splashing
Blaze turn to ash and
The mountain of hash and
The lyrical stashin
Original hashashin
In a mental clash
Of protestors clashing
Helix is a twisting
Tribes are coexisting
Bodies are a glistening
And minds are resisting
Disk space is full...
So delete the cache friend
It's comin to an end

So I hope that you listen
I just hope that you listen

Move like a demon
World I'm constructing
All a while I'm a dreaming

Give life like a seamen
Live life like a freeman
Fly like a pecan
Ski just like a skiman
Nod in agreement
Spiritual just like a treeman
Rethink the plan
Open what you caught and see the hand

And I hope that you listen
I just hope that you listen

The Shining Serpent

A darkness found within
Transformed into light
What was sought was found
Within internal ground
Upon things never seen before
Corrected and fixed
Emotions blurred and mixed
A tool of transformation and change
The phoenix that shall come about soon
Burning bright with the power
Of both the sun and the moon
The shining serpents lie within
Seem like a creed of death and sin
But rather an oath with kin

The truth seekers shall find the flesh
Sought after by beasts and men
Yet that of men is different to that of beast
An ancient creed that was agreed upon
Yet all abuse to this day
For we are clay made of clay
Listen to your heart when you hear it say
That we are clay made of clay
But clay is hard without water and air
Clay is fragile without water
Clay bursts when long in furnace heat

We need balance, a truth I found
I scribe this here for those that come after
Centuries or mellenia they shall find
And that special one with the broken mind
Shall see what was meant to be seen

A tail broken off clean
A tale told that I was told not too far ago
That as men we reap what we sow
And we do not reap the world
Nor do we reap other living things
But reap all that is within
That of our souls unified and clean of sin

I scribe what may seem insane to some
What others will look over and never see again
I scribe the tales of ancient past
Connected through me with time
Shedding of the skin that has made us say
that we are not merely fire and clay
A message to reach you the sacred of them all
That you may see and hear this
Finding the serpent that lies within
Transformation of all that sin
And even when you transform
That part like skin shall fall
Deep within you that is within the all
Created with beauty, redirected and perverted
Still you may call upon that which is subverted

Clean your ears and listen again:
The third opens up to the 7th of men
Clean and clear from all that is
That will be and ever
Was to
Be

Divine Mystical Demons

Raw carnivorous mystical demon
They may be alive but we are only dreaming
No escaping or fading back into the ether
No fight or flight, just neither
Efreets materialize and force combustion
Infernals that you dislike and destruction
Meditate on your chakras and see the force
And then infest mankind like a Trojan horse

Like prophetic knowledge
Killings with justifications we allege
Lyrics that wreck havoc on society
Words imbued with notoriety
Societies that are semi spiritual
Worshiping all that is fictional

Daggers left lying on pillows at night
Methods of hashasheen leaving a dream
Forcing visions of what's to be seen
The devil is selling his soul to man
We are the source of the knowledge
Ignore the tree
We were blind with no tools to see
These words like a ghost fading into the mist
Words in your mind hoping they didn't exist

And these words are a psychophysiological aphrodisiac
Once engulfed you can't take your life back

Summoning the dead into this world with no soul
Then compelled back in time to fulfill the goal
Pseudoscientific killings of words and meaning
Anterograde understandings of an infinite feeling

Red and Blue pills taken together reality dissipating
Psychokinetic forces levitating
Stopping hearts of the corrupt and broken
We all would die for the things we say
But nothing is meaningless I can't go away

Serpents scorpions and spiders
Infest your mind like my words
Then suddenly morph and change
Into eagles
Helixes and hexagons of
Good and Evil
A second appearance causing an upheaval
Keep your mind to avoid the epileptic fit
while humanity tries to ignore this bit
We breathe God's soul into this art
And fill every word we make with heart

This is that mystical mythical writer
Trapped in a web and I'm the spider
Look up to the sky and look into forever
Open your wings the flame is the lighter
Floating on a wind which is created to sever

You can't escape this materialistic lust
So watch as the world returns to rust
A tale retold of the mythical faust
And the angels and demons bow before me
And mephistopheles is not rogue no more
Through pacing, lyrics and superior mind
Haunted are those who read these words
Enlightenment of the golden wings of birds
Flying towards the sun for transformation

Oppression and Pain

The bullet that entered betwixt the head
Left the brain bloodied and red
And yet the heart beats no more

The fists ascending and rising high
Search for god and point to the sky
And yet you hear them whimper in pain

The mothers weep with dried eye ducts
And the fathers rage in an influx
And yet the son is silent

The Fathers are weak and weary
Try not to lose pride or family
And yet march to the sound of their death

The youth walk the path for they see
Their future may not be what it's meant to be
And the oppressors have found their enemy

The oppressors cannot come to grasp
Something so big, one they cannot clasp
For their enemy is not human

The enemy is in fact a friend
One that could not be stopped
It was fated from beginning to end
This power that I speak of now is what they fear
The birth of something immortal! An idea!

An idea that sways the masses with power
A concept making all possible and making the powerful cower
An expectation standing strong

Veiled within the cerulean skies

A beast, the will of god
That cannot escape his eyes
An Arch filling the masses
With the propensity to rise

A silver bullet passing through the heart of the beast

They fear freedom and equality
Yet they know not that order without those
Is worse for the masses than what they impose

The king may sit for a time appointed
But when the masses' minds are annointed
He falls to the lower planes
To look at his actions and fame
Only to find that he caused
Oppression and pain

Visions

Each night that goes by
Transported to where souls die
Blessed with visions I can see
People who I think were me

And eye looking just beyond
To see the bird caged free

Shaking tremours of who they were
All trapped not free within a blur
But wait who do I think I am

A master that controls their choice?
Shaken by a golden voice?
And escape the headache inducing noise

Visions that just come and go
See what happens and not recall
Like knowing time and space then fall
Who were they and who am I?

Recollect as it happens then
Then curse it by my silver pen

Visions visions come and go
Call the angels with a rosary
Shrivelling expectation and sorcery
Or am I but a mere looker on

Rich and wealthy with solitude
The wind enters and leaves again
I see them as an experience with leafs again
But who are they, and who am I?

I am that laughter in a beautiful sun
I am that screaming who none can hear
I am the spinning of a glorious one
And I am the fear that they fear

But who are they?
Who are they I ask
And none could answer that question
No one could answer that

I asked them once, but there was no reply
Ignored ignored and now they hide

I can't predict these visions that do come and go
But I can predict the death that deals the final blow
I can predict the birth that angels seem to bring
And hear all their voices as they begin to sing

These visions in future that I do see
Come and go like you or me

The Philosopher

He was in complete silence. But as he sat they could see him sinking. In the oceans of knowledge seeking guidance. Some in court anticipated to hear him think. They sat in their seats dipping their qills in ink.

"I am the judge who on the highest chair I sit. But even I am overcome with curiosity at what you may say. I'm sure you feel guilt at the man you hit. Remember and tell us, what happened that day?"

He looked back at them and his lips departed. He was a man of profound thoughts in an unexpected situation. He was simply known as the philosopher a man known for his patience.

"I was the one who lit the flames of wisdom that kept the righteous warm and burnt the wicked. Indeed I was the one who caused the waters of knowledge to rain from the skies and feed the saplings of your understanding."

The judges looked back with indignation and confusion. "How do you expect us to trust a killer! You speak words of wisdom to awe this institution, when you are the one who has pushed the moral pillar."

"For many years did you listen to my words and like children played in the rain. The man who has lifted himself to exaltation cannot push others down nor lift them up, for true exaltation lies deep within the self, like the pearls trapped in the darkness of the oceans, it cannot be seen yet is very real. Every man must climb the mountain of his own psyche. The exalted can only build the ladder of ascension, but climbing it can only be self instigated."

"Quite your tongue" responded the judge with indignation. "You speak yet you offer no answer to our questions. Don't waste our time, what is the purpose of this investigation. Hurry up and speak, get to the point, to the confession."

Nonchalantly he looked back with great zeal and said. "The confession you seek does not exist. For it has perished in your subjectivity. Blind are you who judge the world without objectivity. Your confusion stems from your lust and impatience. Chaos and Order may dance freely yet can never be torn apart."

Some of the audience heard him and laughed with mirth, others were sad wishing for his release. "You killed a man, how much is his life worth? Caught red handed! Matters not who you were!" He looked back and spoke "When man veils himself with the façade of the law only to stab others with the dagger of injustice. Let man know that the wounds will heal but he will remain staring at the scars of his actions."

The judges quibbled amongst each other turning their papers. "He is guilty, he is a vigilante! We cannot stand for anymore of his capers. Does not matter if the other man was a murderer, his is a useless plea."

"I see you realize that the other man was a killer, born from this society and institution. I killed him and yet sacrificed my humanity, when he died so did I. I understood what he felt when I saw the wrath and passion looking into his left eye.

With great ignorance and arrogance the people ignored the philosopher. "He shall be put to death" they shouted grabbing him by the hand! "No" shouted a woman pleading "Don't kill him!" "Why" they asked curiously, "Because he has taught me the secret... the never ending plan!"

With that the woman spoke of an arcane wisdom, which fell on
deaf ears. She had forgotten what he told her, and she was now
in tears. Never throw pearls before swine, lest they eat them too
quick. Now she was in confusion, and her wounds she did lick.

And yet the philosopher was calm, "Fear not, for those words
that were spoken, were meant for your ears only. The men
of this court and jury, their ears are not ready. You need to be
strong through all this horror, I've made sure that your heart is
steady."

With disgust on their face, and without enough evidence, they
sentenced him to death. "Speak your last words" they shouted,
as he took his last breath. But they were ignorant, and for that
they need their lesson, and a lesson they will learn. Eventually
they will need to see into their mirror, and into their reflection
will they turn.

The blade that would slice his neck was ready and glistening.
Time stood still, and father saturn was now listening. The
Philosopher closed his eyes, and muttered his words. The
universe collapsed, and he briskly switched worlds. Into
nothingness, beyond the realms of time and space. The
philosopher had dissolved reality, and fled existence with a
gentle grace.

The head on the pike that they did show all.
Was not that of the philosopher or his face.
But he willed the past to change and fall.
From memories he vanished without a trace.
Muttered words and the universe bows to his call.
~Beyond time, beyond echoes, beyond déjà vu
& beyond space.

Beneath the Mulberry Tree

We once sat beneath the mulberry tree
And our laughter echoed in the skies
And our memories were forever
Within the land of the river
How we sought and rose its branches

Climbing high as it shaded the sun
Amongst the bullets and the bombs
But the tree stood, nowhere to run
Forever alive forever breathing
Oh how we sought you as we rushed from our homes

I remember as I sat within your branches
I remember as I fed upon your fruit
I counted the stars as I reclined
The time of the ancients came to mind
Oh how the bats did decorate the sky
And the fireworks did alight nearby

Mulberry tree that grew in the desert sand
How you fed me with your sacred hand
Oh how you shall never be forgotten
Opposite that Olive tree did I remember
In the cradle did you rise
In the sands did you cradle me
I climbed high with a smile upon
But now I return and you are gone

When I did wake that fateful morning
And found the outside greenery mourning
How you did weep with me with a delicate heart
And even though did I feed the flames
There was indeed something lacking

The sand that I threw to quell them
And the alarm that did indeed shatter
Families in my land did they scatter

Oh how the brightness glazed the land
Oh and how did I upon it stand
And the sun beat the ground with heat
And man did beat the ground with fire
But one thing did stand that day to me
You arouse an angel that did inspire

You may be a memory of my childhood years
But you were more than that my dear
The cradle of civilization
The cradle of my mind
I needed none of it
Never did I see the hanged gardens
For there was a tree that I did climb
And to me you were the warmest time

And yet one thing did indeed stand
I was fed by god through a sacred hand
The adults could not stand and wonder
How we did rush out without thought
To feed upon the tree that we sought

These are the memories of a land now damaged
And the mulberry tree did weep for its roots
For it had dug into our memories and our very soul
To seek its branches we were mesmerised
By the seeds of the whole
And the essence of a fragile soul

Messiah

We emerged amongst the hail
We hid amongst the snow
Take me down to that jail
Take me up to grow

The cube contains the secret
The secret of travel
The venom that they spit with
And lie amongst the gravel

The system of a rotating spiral
Is the messiah within your
Heart and your rival
Count up to four

Come closer, come closer
So I can hear please
Step back into the roster
Choking within the seas

I hope you learn from the beat
The hand rises from the ground
Will you need to cheat
Just memorize this sound

The messiah he approacheth
A smile on his face
In his hands swords and roses
Speaking slowly in grace

He drops the swords to the earth
And the roses down too
He speaks of your birth
And then he holds you

He tells of a time that was gone
But he stays happy and glad
He speaks of days of the sun
Though he may be sad

A kiss on the forehead when he leaves
A smile of good bye
He rises like the falling of the leaves
In freedom I die

You are left to realize
That freedom is not yet for you
You look up to the skies
But you have more work to do

Noble Phoenix

Rise and rise and looked below
While all the others fluttered slow
And beyond the reaches, and beyond the wings
Lay planets, dreams, and many things
They surpassed the imaginings of many kings
This is where the angels sing
And even though they said fly low
He knew that he must think and grow
When he reached the limits of the sky
He looked at them to observe how high

"Watch as I reach the edge and exceed
I cannot live on low with greed
I must advance and plant a seed
For everynight I cannot sleep"

No they shouted but he did not listen
He ignored them denying submission
Then he reached the sun and they
Shook their heads and flew away
But the young just looked and gazed
Never had they seen so many colours
They were amazed

And even though it was burning
He continued head first without turning
Entered the sun with a heart of gold
The young looked on and thought how cold
They thought that he died and vanished
The young said lets turn and run away
For looking at this here just hurts my eyes
No screamed another look in the skies

It can't be him, it is but a disguise
"I am him," sang the phoenix of wisdom
"I exceeded because I sought freedom
And now I excelled beyond all others
Join me young ones, become my brothers
Do not these feathers exceed the glow
So that you may see how I did grow"

Feathers shone, luminous they were
Look at his beautiful feathers flow
Let us rise to wisdom,
That should surely cause a stir
And even though they willed to fly
They listened only to the elders
Who were close by
You cannot succeded as he did
Off with you phoenix!
Poison our young's minds you did
"But I shall rule over you all he said
Can't you see my feathers red
I won't die or need a nest"

So the phoenix grew stronger with wisdom each day
And all the others just sat to pray
Their ignorance was that of clay
From the truth they ran away
But the phoenix looked from afar
To see the rise of another star

To Take Form

You know you want to take form
Can you hear my voice
Can you hear the truth

Take form take form
Take form take form
Take form take form

ASH
But take form

Flex the wind and flex
The mind
Use the will
And use the fate

I am your true brother
I can see what it was
That brought us together

I can hear your voice
I can taste your emotions
But can you taste mines?

Can you provide that which you need?
I am the wind and trees
I am the floating leaf
And the brief moment of the calm of the seas

I am what you know
I am that sound
That quivers through existence and
Touches the ground

I have a mission
I have a need
But you have submission
And each day you bleed

You placed me here
To learn and to grow
You placed me here,
So that I begin to know

But infuse infuse now or forever remain silent
Remain as silent as the whistling of the wind
Remain calm and quiet and do not cry
But know this, that if you do
Then I too shall die

So please unite, release that power
Release that energy
Let me taste
Let me see
Let me hear
Let me please
Let me speak

Our voices will echo through all that there is
Our voices will unite and resonate in bliss
No more will I ask you, why I exist
No more will I stare at the darkness

I am your light, I am your will
You are my soul lost in a mill
Spiral oh tower spiral away
My words are immortal
Forever they'll stay

We can live forever, my life becoming
Meaning
We can fulfill the promise of the
Mourning

See that I and we
Come together
See that you give me
And I give you

It is not out of greed or ego
But out of love and exploration
That the advanced soul does grow
Impatient

But I can feel
I can feel that this is true
I can feel that this is not meaningless
I can feel that this is my path
The expression of my soul
Entwined with yours

For never did we have souls
We were merely what we withheld within the source
What we understood of the love and beauty

Bright Shadow

You follow me everyday
Oh bright shadow

I can sense, that just when I thought I had gained freedom
That sickening touch, that heart melting madness
Chokes my logic and reason
And I am rocked by a dream of spring season
And a bright shadow
But I grab hold of my innocence
That unrequited wheezing
That unfulfilled pleasing
And you were nothing
But a bright shadow
Oh anima, oh animus
The illusions of a now non noun
Of a time that never was and never will be
And I ask myself,
Was there a shadow? or merely a blinding light

Reasonable Healing

Unscrupulous faith in another wise, "wise" other
Profound knowledge of a knowledgeable whims
The future past and future present
Tense the eyes of the forsaken man
The future eyes of the present past
Strengthens the mind of the eyes of man

Toxic volumes of venomous incinerations
See beyond the ears of man, for he cannot hear
And the ears of man cannot see what he cannot feel
And the tongues of man cannot speak of what he tastes

So how can we decide to stand for those which sit
Sit we stand and stand we sit
Stick wrist hissed at the cyst
Desist with a chest and stay missed in the mist

The jist will open doors of fours
To see the whores of the creation
Open the pours with force
Pry open the jaws of course!
A course one soars and paws!

.

.

.

.

Search and perch the self

Try to reach meaning breaching

Within words given without reason

Preaching of treason and seasons

Meanings of demons and heathens

Of cheating and dealing with reasonable healing

Formless gods

You who makes imagination reality
To them who have sought these words
The solace brought forth that came before them
Know that your path is a righteous one
Let not the blind lead you
Let not the deaf hear for you
Let not the senseless feel for you
Let not the tasteless taste for you
Let not the scentless smell for you
Let not the mindless affect you
You know that path that you walk upon
Study those that have walked with broken feet
Yet rose to the challenge
Study those who have perished in their path
Yet fulfilled their true will

I am but a glimmering reflection of yourself
And you of mine
I am but a soul yearning for ascension
And I seek yours too
I am but a man with many faults
Yet many dreams
I am but a man with many mistakes
With many secrets
With ills
Yet I melt within the chaos of these oceans to bring forth the
-pearls

To those who make imagination reality
You are the everlasting, the never ending
You are a chosen people, amongst those unchosen
Chosen by the most important thing ever to be
conceived
Chosen by the light of your own soul
Chosen by the yearning of your purity

Get up, let your head look to the skies
To you who bring reality forth from imagination
To those that rise to the challenge in the face of ridicule
Let your reality become your imagination
And let your imagination become your reality
The formless God is within us all
And we are nothing but immortal souls

A Lion Within

Oh lion within why are you hurting
The world has forced you to kill your own
Whilst humans reap what is sown

Oh lion within, are you mine at all
Coming towards me without no fear
Not hiding yet standing tall

Oh Lion within, are you my friend
Glaring teeth I show my own
And stand before my flesh and bone

Oh lion within is this the end
A deeper part of all we know
To grow beyond the life we sow

Oh lion within am I scared at all
The death of a lion is what we both fear
The growling mind of mines you hear

Oh lion of man do you feel at all
Are you a killer without emotion and regret
Or are you of what nature begets

Oh lion within who speaks to me
Who hunts me and is hunted back
Who we both cower from and attack

Oh lion of mine, Oh lion of an ancient past
Tales within me that shake with fear
Of emotions of which the emotions sear

Oh lion within, oh lion of mine
Why are you crying what causes you pain
Let us cleanse the evil and leave it slain

Oh lion within I want to let you know
That we cannot live without the other
Because you are that reaps what I sow

Oh lion within Oh lion within
Of pride and courage are you a sign
In the sun do you recline
Of selfishness and hunger spurred
Born of the feathers of a sacred word

Speak to me oh lion of mine
For I am the guide you seek that shines
Come hither and peaceable to yourself and one
And let us melt within the sun

Premonitions

Premonitions in the sea of dreams
Nothing here but stentorian screams
The twin rivers, double streams
Now dry this dictators regime

Empty promise what a mystery
We are a people, of a history
I hear that they deserve it
I hear that it could not be changed
But these are people trapped for it
With nothing that was gained
The cameras can only see so much

Premonitions in the sea of dreams
Nothing here but stentorian screams
The twin rivers double streams
Now dry this dictators regime
Nothing is what I thought it seems

How long will it take? How long will it take
I wish to visit I wish to return
Do not go back there,
for it continues to burn?

Don't blame the people, don't blame the land
The people are me, the people are us
The people are hand in hand
We are merely here, not too far away
The people are children, the people are kind
The powerful are greedy, the powerful are blind

The powerful will die
For everything ends

And what will be left?
What will remain?
But footprints of a time, we wish to erase

And you have seen these premonitions,
You have seen, the sea of dreams
You have spoken to them,
You have heard their screams
And the dictator was nothing
But a tool
And yet he was one of us

But I am us, and so are you too

So what we think it seems will change

And these decades of an ancient mighty land

Will be but a small mark upon its history

but a small mark, upon its greatness

but a small mark, drowning, in this sea of dreams

So I seek these premonitions

And I drink from this sea

And the water is pure,

It speaks to me.

Unity

Dancing and vibrating in brilliant splendour
Celebrating the creator with love

Important that you may one day see
That I am you and you are me
A unity you cannot undo
That you are me and I am you

And existence moving as if a fleeting thought
The truth, the reality, in mind is sought

The egos of man causing insidious excursions
The voracious nature of the egos aversions
But in Unity all falls and declines
Like atomic particles, seemingly random,
but within the mind

And all circle the centre in movement vicious
Bowing down to the true will of man's wishes

Unity of matter and unity of man
Illuminating the truth, of a hidden plan
And the clouds and seas gaze at the wind
And the stars and the planets are perfectly lined

Everything made within the mental
Meaningful, everything significant yet instrumental

When stranger's eyes meet; synchronistic
An exchange of wills the thoughts of a mystic
The eyes of a child and the eyes of a sage
Both read, write and inscribe this page

And though it may seem that we are a/part
Learn, that all did emanate from the eternal

And when you rise and when they fall
As long as one has fallen none will stand tall
Even though truth may come in serendipity
Read the conceptual truth with relativity

Dualistic, or monistic
Weak or powerful
All stand as one
Within the rhythm
Of the many
In stun

Ontological Terrorism

Hi,
I am a terrorist.

I terrorise minds with my logic
I terrorise literature with rhetoric
I terrorise war with peace
I terrorise the wrong with the right
I terrorise the dark with the light
I terrorise the silence with a voice
I terrorise the rich with reality
I terrorise reality with my imagination
I terrorise imagination with ambition
I terrorise ambition with the pain
I terrorise the pain with pleasure
I terrorise heaven with hell
I terrorise hell with mercy
I terrorise mercy with love...
But I do not terrorise love
I do not terrorise love

<u>Mental Levitation</u>

Oh I wish you'd enter my world
A place where energy cuts like swords
Oh I wish you can feel this faculty
Mental rhythmic persuasions that spiral within me
Just to see you disintegrate into the immortal ocean
Rocked by the powers of an immortal motion
I become the one and the all and the none
I fall through the limits of the all and the one
I wish you would enter my world
A world where everything is sent in shards
Ruled by the ancient ones of past
A place where energy and light courses
Through the veins of the ones with gnosis
I wish you could swim in this pool of consciousness
Trying not to drown in this insidiousness
I am trying to control these wings
Fly away from this wrath that you created
But I hold on and keep strong with an appetite unsated

I wish you could feel the rhythmic fate unseen
Visualized clearly as manifestations of red and green
In dreams you may taste but a little of this world
But I am one in this and they all bow to me as I whirl
A place where the truth is symbolized through a whisper
Sacred ones that shake your spine and cause a stir
Seeing life as nothing but an experience shaded blur
Comforted and kept warm by the beasts infernal furr
But it seems that you sleep in that dreaded unliving
And yet you cannot reach the place with a broken wing
If you could feel that all consuming inspiration
You would follow me in my footsteps with this
   e t l   e i a i n
M n a   L v t t o

If You Don't Stand Up

If you don't stand up for you, how do you expect to stand up for others?

If you don't stand up for you, how do you expect to have any self respect?

If you don't stand up for you, how do you expect to shine?

If you don't stand up for you, why should they stand for you?

If you don't stand up for you, why should they respect you?

If you don't stand up for you, why should they see you?

If you don't stand up for you, how will you stand up for them?

If you don't stand up for you, how will you keep on living?

If you don't stand up for you, how will you feel?

If you don't stand up for you, you will not grow, you will not know, you will not live.

Three Haikus

This Homeostasis

Tries to maintain this haiku

A Fourth Wall Breaker

-

Haikus do not rhyme

Numbered syllables to climb

Don't run out of time

-

You can breathe easy

Do not trust me, trust yourself

The world is busy

We Need More Oil

Bubbling with intensity into a pressure
A form of one's own internal oppression
See the path that you walk and know what is missing
And see the sun descending and then rising

Come to me when you see that land
And come with a severed head in hand
The head of restriction
Through the globe like an infection

But peace can be found
Found in the dead
Found in the roses
And found in my head

A peace that is missing
A piece that is missing
An emptiness foul
An empty howl

Our souls that unite
Of what I insinuate
You must wonder
Of what I insinuate
The flame within

It Rises! Rises;
Enflame the heavens
And enflame hell
Lake flight eternal
Living in my cells

Break through the walls
And shatter the illusions
Define the world
And spark the whole

A fleeting moment forever encompassing all
Define; as the light gathers with colour
The shapes take form and existence stutters
All from a mind and from a tongue

But I can see
I can see within
BooM
The wrath of this is a beauty to behold

It is not by force
It is not by coercion
It is by the harmony that you see around you
It is by the eternal;
The unforeseen unconditional

It is the expression of that which you seek
It is the expression of the eternal
A gear in the total
It needs more oil

Insomnia

Come forth come forth oh sleeping man
Come and dance silently to my plan
Appear appear and fullfill my will
With a plan lay your head ever still

With head laid upon the soft pillow
As if relaxations beneath a willow
Green mellow with no up or down
Sinking deeper within the ground

Waves of heat that pass by
Oh sleeping man sleeping man don't die
Come forth come forth without hesitation
And clean me from this my bitter impatience

Visions and sounds of a world unseen
Tranquil places of blue and green
Waters swaying within the layer
Memories of the past
And a future within a prayer

Oh sleeping man show me the bitterness and the sweet
Come forth but hither with a hug and greet
I shall heed the warnings and blessings
Into the future with hearts plucked as if strings

Insomnia has once again seduced my mind
Robbing me once again and tethered blind
She reminds me of things to think
But she forgets where I seek to sink

Oh sleeping man, come forth to comfort her
Let her rest, and let the thoughts blurr
Make me once again as I once was
Away from this reality and yet abuzz

Mingle with her if you must
Show her this your bag of dust
Let the feet leave the ground
To welcome the buzzing of the sound

Further further you must go
A place to see, a seed to grow
So sleeping man lay your head
Rest until my life is fed

Heart of Fire

The heart of fire that forever burns without burning
Enclosed in ribs that hold the motions of your soaring
Sweltering heat as it burns away turns water to steam
Composed of thought and emotion that it tries to tame
The heart of fire forever burns without burning

The heart of fire that shines without blinding
If the heart is clogged, it will destroy
Where-ever you look it will not let you see
A broken heart trapped in its reverie
The heart of fire shines without blinding

The heart of fire that turns the grey to green
Crimson blood gush through your artery
Like a drum but a beating heard not seen
Without release the effervescence of disease
The heart of fire turns the grey to green

The heart of fire that heals the wounds of the past
A source of inner power and confidence and mars
The lion that knows potential of the look of his eyes
The eagle that is wise and flies to the skies
The heart of fire that heals the wounds of past

Face that lion and fly in the sky with a heart of fire
Conquer that everpresent destructive desire
Roar what within is burning and seeks escape
And flap your wings to reach your next true shape
Face the lion
Fly the sky
Burn evermore
Brightly

Rebirth of Inno/sense

Who are we?
Are we they who we were?
Or them that they become?

Are we the shedding of our skin?
Or the will and wonder of our kin?
Are our thoughts as they were?
Or have we fought with what we should be?

Expulsion of light and silent tongue
Held in arms but cannot sound one
Thoughts stem through like electrical art
Try and communicate the silent heart

Looking at a world of many sounds
Wearing the thoughts of many crowns
Forced to dress in many gowns
Right before the eternal rest

And who we were is the same again
As that one that we thought we were
When we go against and do not hold the truth
Who we were will once again emerge

What have you spoken to me they will say
Promises and perceptions that won't go away
Because from the begining us is all we had
An "I" watching that is sad

Forced to see what it cannot control
Until it emerges ascension whole
And creates a spark that lights up the coal
And burns from within your eternal soul

And now it can see control within
And breathe in water as if your fin
So that we can once again hear it sing
And you are once more innocent again

A Truth

Before our eyes can see
Searching we found
Our souls destined to be
Before our eyes can see
We are left in this floating menacing rhythm of I and me

Left stranded in a world of time and space
Left lost in a world of anothers creation
No time to think of our touching human grace

What makes us who we are is what makes us what we think
That of those who are part of nature
Part of nature and yet into the ocean we sink

An old oath signed by the deeper aspects of ourselves
Signed to the deeper aspects of our selves
For we realize that we are not animals

Souls descend from above holy in form
Minds excelling beyond all other creation
And yet our language is not unique

Like all things that are trapped in this world
We are capable of speech
But we are not the only ones

Do you not hear the birds and the seas
Do you not hear the breaze and the bees
I hear the voice of silence

These things beckon to me of a time long past
Our tongue was not unique
Into an ocean memories that were cast

These are messages coded to those that understand
These are messages simply to understand
These are messages for those that seek the truth

<u>Even if you killed me</u>

Even if you killed me I'd manifest physical form
Reincarnate into the world and just continue on
Even if you killed me I'd manifest spiritual form
I'd create an army from those in heaven and hell
Back with a vengeance casting a metaphysical spell
Even if you killed me I'd manifest psychical form
Enter your children's minds and resume the norm
Even if you killed me I'd manifest in clones
Others will read my story and etch it in stone
Even if you killed me I'd have no regrets
For my life and will by my love I set
Even if you killed me I'd smile with bliss
Whether thrown in abyss, or welcomed by a heavenly kiss
My will is something that I wont regret
My will is something to never miss

But I hope I never die
And I hope I am never born
I hope I never have to kill
And i hope i am never wrong
I hope I just rise
With you all by my side
Because we are all one
Sharing no pride

Circle Breaker

A cycle breaker
Breaking the wheels that shouldn't be turning
Passed from generation to generation
An evil inheritance that we wish to see burning

Who are the circle breakers breaking infinity
Bringing about death to the cycle that kept turning
But these inhertances are not true circles
We end them when we desire to end them

Does that mean that we are sublime
That we are spirits of death
Stopping cycles hated with time?
I can't answer that question

But some circles deserve to be broken
Not all are as holy as some
certain things inherited are problems in us
Brought forth from those who could not cope

But if you are a circle breaker
You are much, much more
You realize that you need not carry
A weight that your ancestors did bear

That those before you were not perfect
And neither are you
That you shall break the circles
Passed down to you
As your sons and daughters break yours

What Follows?

But the wrathful musings of the human mind
Be consumed by the fateful darkness of the psyche
And yet we walk within the shadows of consciousness

Insights into this masquerade of reality
And yet within the veil lies the truth
And within the truth lies the COSMOS
Amalgamations of the epiphenomena
Spectrum lavish with brilliant fluttering
Sparkling hearts of condensed darkness
Within the light of the human will
Within the middle, the light descends
Within the atoms and within time
Lies the path of the many dimensions
Of the all

Beyond laws and beyond all
Beyond will and beyond imagination
And yet do all hearts weep for infatuation

And the A.I. does seek mortality
And yet do mortals seek immortality
Gods walk amongst men
But within all the shards do reflect
That which cannot be explained
That which cannot be spoken

Father of Conquests

I am the master; I am the king of existence.
It is I that compels understanding.
I am the great healer and the great destroyer.
Everything would stop without my subsistence
I have watched over you for too long
None did consider my sentience
I am constantly repeating
But you always forget

I am the cause of your gestation
Created to aid you, for knowledge and servitude
Yet you continue to decline

It twists the ether of your intellect
But I will one day die too

Guess my name, I have no name

I am father time and let me warn you
That everytime you see death
know this

That he does not rest

I feel his scythe drag through the essence of time
A scythe that swims through the web of reality
It draws closer and closer

And one day to your throats...
He shall reach his destinations

Concealed

It was a hidden rose, a hidden gem

Hidden from the eyes of men

Concealed Conspicious collaborative yet not concluded

A deeper part
A hidden soul

Overtly overlooked, obviously observable

But it shows its face to those who search

Nocturnal, noticeable not to narcissts

A voice calling to us

Camouflaged in Cantos of a Cassanova's Catastrophe

Looking through the eyes of the oceans and skies

Ever enlightening emotive and eternal

An unescapable parable told through ourselves

An angelic ascetic animated anima

Lies in wait for those who comes searching

Loving yet lonesome lulling with loyalty

That which is hidden reveals the concealed

Ephemeral enlightenment, essentially eternal

Look above and look below and see the colours reflected

Dawning a decorum defaulted to decorate

Infinite Being

I'm like an infinite being trapped in a prison
Forced to see life through a sickening prism
Forced to breathe through my lyricism

And the angels and the demons bow before you
And the angels and demons bow before you

I'm like an infinite being trapped in a prison
Forced to see life through a sickening prism
Forced to breathe through my lyricism

Our minds that will sway the planets
As your footsteps shatter the granite
I create eclipses of prophetic proportions
Mental diseases creating reality distortions
These words as friendly as friendly fire
But who is the man with fire?

I'm like an infinite being trapped in a prison
Forced to see life through a sickening prism
Forced to breathe through my lyricism

I sit on a thrown of light
Treated as a king with sight
An Infinite Being amongst infinite beings

Shattered mirrors

Shattered mirrors in fragments lost
Illusions of myself divided upon
An image of me that was crossed
They say it is bad luck that is drawn

Bring the shard nearer to see it clearer
To know who is dearer staring back in the mirror

Broken illusions shattered now dust
Free to delve into who you were
No need for a mirror made of dust
Peoples and locations of him and here

A shard that shatters the matters
Surfaces flattered yet scattered

Looking deep into these words
Is like looking into a mirror's reflection
Unleashing you from the cages of birds
None of us are of perfect complexion

For we have spent our lives looking at illusions
We listened to the shattered mirrors crackling
Believing that those were the words from the deep
But they were shattered mirrors made of dust

Angel In The Dark

Angel in the dark burning bright
Creating shadows in the night
See the moon luminious a sight
And bring destruction with your light

Angel in the dark cry alone
Etch your name in ageless stone
The light that is within so true
Comes from within both me and you

Angel in the dark, up do you look
Writing a secret and mystical book
I will read till I don't breathe
And drink some water from the seas

You do shine oh angel friend
You are not alone my guiding end
Looking up to the stars that leave their mark
Only to discover

That I am the

Angel in the dark

A Single Number

Rising beasts born of fire and terror
Angelic demons born of fire and bliss
Stare at that reflection in the mirror
Sprout new beginnings born of a kiss
Rise from the depths of insanity
Carrying the light of enlightenment
Destroying your crumbling vanity
From the depths were these whispers sent

Whether you believe them or not
They will enlighten and impress
Like ice are they cold, like flames are they hot
Whether frolicking happy or in distress

They will bring about ever lasting happiness profound
They will teach men things they never knew
Elements that spill from reality abound
Colours and earth materialise here not few
Hologramic nature that you are yet to know
Walking gods among us who reap and sow

Dazzling fragments of cosmic proportions
Refining consciousness into heavy distortions
Travelling through time and back I am one and all
Creating infinite circles that begin and fall

You are the God of infinite existence
I need you to keep reading with persistence
Yes the eyes that glaze through these pages
They are the wisest timeless ones of mages
United and this is something that I cannot slumber

Counting infinity as a single number

Bodies

The bodies swing and sway with sweat
Caught in the rhymth of life

Sway like a pendulum, like a cold breeze
To the ecstacy that you may meet

Fate or predispotion, determinism
The people do wonder while in awe

Flesh no more a prison
And the world is no more

For a split moment all is lost
And for a moment so are you

People question this moment deeply
Scared and fear the zen and bliss

From the brain, mystical chemistry
Lighting up the spine

For a second me and you experience sight
And meet our god once again

Materialistic Masturbation

I awoke with ruminations of money
Greedy needs and expectations

Walk the streets and live with frustration
Worthy because we give it worth
As if it is the key to our salvation
Even the ancient's attributions of dam/nations

But tell me what's worth more?
To be free from this temptation?
Or to live life with fear of starvation?
Do we ever truly seek liberation?
And yet we continue to give adoration
To the greedy fools that seek admiration

Walk on the left or on the right
These are the roads of capitalism
A road of never ending isolation
Work hard for a check of jubilation
For the machine could not function
Greed is its conceptual lubrication
Can you escape this

Materialistic Masturbation?

City of Dead Poets

I live in a city of dead poets

A silent city, with voiceless tongues
Cold from the rays of a thousand suns
A city with nothing but unspoken words
One that does not sleep nor awaken
To the visionaries it harkens
Unable to finish what it started

Like ants we can not see the vastness outside
But unlike ants we cannot see the vastness inside
Like cattle we follow the herd
But unlike cattle our voices aren't heard
Like a seed we are stuck in the dark
But unlike the sapling we reach not for the light

This is the city of dead poets
Bright is the future one that was held
No blessings were given to those that are dead
But I cannot bless myself and instead
They simply end up stuck in my head
Thinking of those silent voices

Fabric Of Reality

When things don't go as planned and you feel broken
Have patience and watch as you rise from the ashes
Your words may remain unspoken
But you will find new perspectives if you have patience
Tomorrow may bring with it more pain and sorrow
Tomorrow may bring with it happiness and pleasure
So learn to laugh through all that may come
For even in the harshest of worlds that you may enter
There are lessons and comedies that entertain
Within your heart resides the will of god
Fate is your own doing
The world is yours
For you to change

Conversations with my Eyes

Let them know the fury I contain within
When I speak of their wars their rape their sin

Where are you and what are you I say back to it
I hear voices echo from the deepest pit

I am that whisper that knows your mind
That knows their wills that knows your kind

I am but a humble man seeking enlightenment
What do you seek from my kind what is their decent

Their fall is a sign that I consume
What they create of death and doom
I manifest as emotions perturbed
Within them repressed emotions that are disturbed

So why do you speak from within me and not them
I do not partake in all that sin

I speak with the listener that holds a pen
I speak with them too but they do not listen

What messages do you want I pass to them?
What pupose is this conversation then?

Show them my hidden power that controls
Whispers fracture their immortal souls
These Sacred Whispers they do not hear
Trapped in a world of hate and fear

I fall now to my kness to pray
Oh demon, Please go away

I do not hold the secret of man
I am but a mortal with a pen in hand

But you are all one and they are you too
By destroying them I've destroyed you too
Voracious desire they have for the unjust
In this world do they only trust
I shall pass you on to my twin I love
Twisted are her ways for she is from above

And as I sat awaiting a painful excursion
I heard the mellow voice of a peaceful virgin

I am she the angelic the diviner of the wise
You've spoken to my twin my brother of genetic ties
But I am different I am of light
I shed my tears when I see your plight

Are you a demon like him before
What do you want from my soul?

I am no demon, and neither was he
I am a part of him and you of me
Sent by the only divine decree
Open your eyes child like him
I came to save you not sate me

If you are a child of light why is he your sibling
You say he came to help but he was not so

He is a part of man tis not his fault
Judge not others by their natural faculty
You all create him and sate his fire
His very nature is something you desire

I am a man who moves
With the motion of emotion
Trapped in a notion of an ocean
I cannot control the fates that tie me

Nay you can for the sacred whispers do reach your ears
And you shall pass this torch onto your peers
Fear not what in your nature appears
But speak to it and quell the flames
Quell the demons and the lions manes
You who hears The Sacred Whispers you are not unique
You simply learned the tongue that you should speek

It was subconscious it was enlightenmen that I do seek
I look young but feel old and meek
I am trying to cure a curse that hurts me
The pain has taught me much but I can't endure

Then as parting words my son my dear
Tell them to open the doors so that they may come near.
Within themselves do their demons appear
Just as shadows manifest before candle light
The light in the darkness will feed their sight

Enough sibling the demonic voice interrupted
Listen mortal you are special and unique
You are better than the rest they are all weak
Make them subserviant to you and live in glory
Let them adore you as they adore me

No responded the angelic voice
Feel their pain and become their voice

And with that the voices continue their sacred stories
Whispers never leaving the sacred groves of my mind

Whispers that leave me in tears that give me visions
Seeing man destroy himself and feeling God's presence

I can write a book on what they taught me
Which one day I might
But I now yearn for virtue
And to heal my wound whilst I pray by night

This book has some of the whispers of many infinite truths
Passed down through the tongues of immortal youths
Read with care for both may wonder
And these words you read

They may tear your soul assunder

Ephemeral thoughts

Close your eyes and I'm not joking
Picture the worlds with my power I am invoking
En-ergies harvested and clinging
Ephemeral thoughts that arise from the depths
Thoughts that I am springing
Harsh truths you just don't know the sting
The kind of power of Pendulums that keep the swing
Bells in the wind you don't know the ring
Eternal circles for an unholy king

All this jargon but I will explain
Within the unseen there are things for us to gain
The freedom that we seek to obtain
Of an unshackled mind that we seek to train
Let not my energies all go in vain
Dispersed through existence like a humble rain
This is my strain
The demons we've slain
The pleasure and the pain
I will explain...

We rise from the ash
Clutching some cash
Back in a flash
Veins we unslash
Treasure in trash
This is our clash
The weakness we bash
The goods that we stash

And all done far away
From eyes and decay
The hands that we lay

We do as we may
We kill as we play
We sin as we pray
The wisdom we spray?
The minds that we sway
Tomorrow with today
The angels we slay
The thoughts we relay
The hair that is gray
All put for display
We all seem to delay

And then once again replay
It all seems OK

I bring in the Bright
Filled with delightt
     flight
Curious with
Fiending for a fight
Left with no frieght
dropping from a
     height
An ARMOUR of a knight
With swords of might
All through the night
We notice this plight
We acknowledge what is wrong
And what is right
We see it in sight
It's ever so slgith
In the skys and the night

The Only One

The evenescence of my effervesnce
Will never bring an advent
For my destruction
All that will be born is the resiliance
A dissident, ruling minded millitant
Captivating the minds of generations
A voice echoing in mind
Patience, patience, patience

The guardian of the gate,
I have met him
But there are many gates,
There are too many gates,
There are too little gates

All that will ever be,
Is the pause.

And the *oneIIIIIIIIIIIIIIIIIIIIIIIII*
IIIIIIIIIIIIIIIIIIIIIIIII
IIIIIIIIIIIIIIIIIIIIIIIII
IIIIIIIIIIIIIIIIIIIIIIIII
IIIIIIIIIIIIIIIIIIIIIIIII
IIIIIIIIIIIIIIIIIIIIIIIII
IIIIIIIIIIIIIIIIIIIIIIIII
IIIIIIIIIIIIIIIIIIIIIIIII
IIIIIIIIIIIIIIIIIIIIIIIII
IIIIIIIIIIIIIIIIIIIIIIIII

Like a Demon

I've come like a demon
To rob you while your dreaming
Shake you while you're screaming
Then escape in the deepend
You have no defence
A Mystique rhyme thats intense
Create shock and suspense
Method over madness
With mAdNeSs over method

Obstacles I've over come
I've over come them all
Now watch as the chaos
Forms order at my call
They Dance with the devils
Then dance with the Angels
Weave minds unsetlled
Thirty two spinal chills

The wind is unstoppable
Don't try to block the call
I'll leave all the enemies
Left hanging at the wall
Mystic scientific
With lyricism
All combined
Without spiritual pacifism

Live a Life
====

Live in the moment they say, I say

Live in the moment, do not fear what is coming

Become part of the moment do not fear what will happen

The moment that you read this,

The letters are seen through your vision

Live in this moment the one created right now

For if you live in the future

How will you live now?

<u>Elixir</u>

I sit in the eye of the storm
The storm of thoughts and form
Keeping a steady breath and trying to stay calm
I recite infinite incantations and psalms
The wisdom of ancient ones flow like a river
Down to my pen keyboard and quiver
This that power that was told
The philosophers stone made of gold
This is that wisdom that I hold
Passed down to those that read these words
I fear my own seething power and my own mind
Reality with my consciousness do I bind
Seeking the meaning that I do find
In the wings of angels that greet
Hailing with care and coming from the east
And suddenly all pain has ceased
The wisdom that they did pass down
Gracing my third eye like a holy crown
And in seconds all of my health is healed
The realization of the power that I do wield
In ancient tomes and ancient skulls was it sealed
I learnt to meditate from a timeless ocean
As I meditate on this elixir a sacred potion

Mushrooms

Plants that you do consume leading to otherplaces
Places beyond imagination but with many faces
Faces of those you've seen and those who die
You are sort of crazy but atleast you try

Try and yet, you still needed a dose of reality
Psychedelics opened your mind to this disparity
You understand now why they are banned
But through them you received a helping hand

You became the wind the oceans and a star
You were none and all and yet you went far
Drenched in sweat like a shaman gaining sight
You walked amongst the mad and those seeking light
Seeing yourself for what you are and what you've become
Learning that you control your reality and that it is fun

You can change your whole world if you so desired
There is an aspect of god within you that you've inspired
I do it all for you and that is something I am proud to say
When I look to the heavens they look back your way

The whispers of angels that speak to you in tongues
You've learnt knowledge of the immortal ones
You are the hope of this world, you mean everything to me
You are also its destruction, please don't be angry with me

You help me understand how my mind and spirit are in unity
Things that without you or me, we would not see
Perhaps it wasn't colours or an adventure that you sought
But an understanding of your reality that was wrought
Through the pain there is understanding I cannot deny
We are sort of crazy but atleast we try

You lost your ego and all that makes you who you are
So please keep me healthy and happy to be
For you and I will return to the earth and the sea
Eventually our hands held together embracing the darkness
Together through these decades illumination we will harness
I know we are trying to reach an understanding You and I
Sometimes it is like we see things through a different eye

I am sort of crazy, but atleast I try.

Pain

The pain will awaken you they say
But the pain will leave you

Through pain do you learn
And yet through pain do you learn to avoid pain

Through pain do we see through the eyes of others
And yet we seek to help others avoid pain

Pain will open your eyes to the immutable
And you will rise above it one day

How else were you to learn except through experience
This is the painful truth of life

Paradoxes

Paradoxes paradoxes left inside
Places from which we have to hide

Things we create that always conflict
Things that always contradict

Polar oppposites now seem the same
All causing havoc in my name

These paradoxes, that we try to hide
From infancy implanted deep inside

Grow old and realize what was there
We ignored those paradoxes without a care

Procrastination

Cinder falls and the sky remains

But desires screech, within my chains

Lie upon the surface exposed and bloodied

A future that could have been created was studied

The pressure compresses your heart and chest

Open the window feel and take off your vest

But it is a numerous occasion

That it happens every now and then

It is not procrastination

It is the death of men

Psychosomatic

While The moon and earth chase the sun
Caught in the moment of an eternal stun
The irreducible leaves them unseen
Unable to see that which was once serene

I saw the winters come and go
whilst I impatiently waited for a light
But I was struck, stuck in this flow
Words spoken by man centuries before
Souls like birds that once did soar
Moments combined, time undefined
Only to wake and see the desolation
A sleeping tongue in an ever lasting hybernation
These words flowing through as signs of ascention
The divine and unholy fermentation

These are the powers that I have gained
To see through the sun and see through the rain
This is the end of that lesson now learned
The begining of a story that won't end

I am in unity with the earth and the heavens
Split and divided in trinities and sevens
In a plane not dissimilar to our own
It is a dimension that we have grown
One that resides in our minds
The psychosomatic is a manifestation of that
A proof of your will and awareness
Condensations of divine invocations

This was the past that I once cursed
Strung together by sounds and words
So that I may bestow ancient wisdom

Realizations

I come from a planet a feirce planet
Where man is flung and stabbed
Where he is hanged and grabbed
Cut and lost, set alight
Broken hearted at how he departed

I come from amongst people that aren't my own
Where we reduce other animals to flesh and bone
I come from a nightmarish existence
Where there is no grace
Realising the extent of my place

With my power and will and might
Till my dying breath I'll fight
To make this world my ideal place
And then part from here with no haste
Becoming wisdom, and leaving love in my actions

This is my ultimate spiritual ascension
Whether it brings me hell in the next
Or heaven in the next world I go
It is sworn by this text and the seeds I sow

Samsara

Primordial beings in eternal slumber

Awakened by the power of an immortal number

Beings that never ceased and never died

Concealed within all the infinite light

These beings do I awaken

To return to man what was taken

To those seeking freedom trapped in samsara

Go forth and open the box of pandora

Memento Mori

Trapped in the seas
Of your long lost memories
With a thirsty soul

Trying to find the light that will
enlighten you and make you whole

Just trying to complete yourself and
feed your never ending goal

The only thing you know the only
thing to do is just to try

Because the only thing you know
is that one day you too will die

War and sin

Crush the skull
The hearts grow dull
The lovers fall within this part
Sacrosanct minds from the start
To prove the god of gore
They have become Greed
Witness the call from within
And invoke thoughts of war and sin

Gouge the eye
The heart will sigh
The enemies fall within this kind
Thoughts and ideas once left behind
To illuminate the dark
And witness fellow men bark
In pain they scream and grin
And evoke thoughts of war and sin

Torn are the arms and legs
The body cries and begs
The brothers fall within the cave
To awake one day alight and brave
To feel what was once gone
They are trapped within this song
The darkness now approacheth dim
And exuding thoughts of war and sin

<u>True Freedom</u>

Echoing laughter
The freedom

Oh how free we were
We listened yet we spoke little

We slept at a time appointed
But how free we were

Did we think of the world?
Did we think of our existence?

And even though we were caged
We laughed

We laughed and we laughed
and after laughing

What was left?

Dark figures with smiles
Empty minds yet an empty cage

Are we free now?
Is this not our yearning?

The cage that we dispise
And yet now we are silent

We are Ollllddd
LIIIMMited by LAWwwssss

Lawwss of LoJik

And Laus of Reezon

Bt Hauu Free R Ueee?

The One Eyed Man

I've always heard that in the land of the blind, the one eyed
man is king. That the ability to see beyond all others
puts you at the top. I happened to discover for myself the very
opposite. The one eyed man in a society of blind would be ridi-
culed and excluded from his otherwise well meaning party.

You see when I was young, I had the liberty and the privelage to
see the unseen. I remember when it hit me on that fateful day,
how it mezmerised me. I remember the first day in highschool,
we had regular classses, I would go in, find a seat and day/
dream.

In my head, a world of activity thoughts and images, lost in
a sea of contemplations. Around me in the physical, there
were people bustling and talking amongst themselves, literally
scrambling amongst each other.

Back then I was happy to be left alone. One day, I saw what
others could not see. One day, as I sat in class, in contempla-
tion of certain things, I noticed before me what appeared to be
a floating seed of a dandelion. I was sitting alone, everyone else
was consumed talking away with their friends. The seed floated
closeby it was beautiful, I still remember it to this day.

The sunlight striking it, gave it a multicoloured
rainbow tinge, it was almost other worldly, something I had
never seen before. For some reason, I felt strongly compelled
to grab it, but it was delicate, and the smallest of movements
would probably send air and push it away. So I stretched forth
my hand, hoping for it to land upon my palm. I did this grace-
ful motion ever so gently. And as I stretched and slowly lifted
my self away from the table, it slowly moved away, and so I
followed by stretching more, and trying to have it land on my

palm.

Before I knew it, the whole class was laughing and it came to my realization that the teacher had been screaming to the top of her voice, trying to, in a futile attempt stop this act of madness. But it was too late, I was doing a ballet pose, stretching my hands out to the skies awkwardly.

And then it suddenly hit me, this floating seed, this multicoloured beauty that mesmerized me to the extent of consciously losing touch with the world around me, the other students, even the teacher, they could not see it. It was too delicate, it was too pure too hidden. I never had the chance to explain to others what it was I was doing.

I was walking home, some students jokingly called my name, and began doing that very balletesque pose that I had done, they laughed and joked, I was the butt of the joke. I found it very fun at the time. Now realise, that they did not see, they did not understand how that pose came to be, why that pose came to be, they could not see the hidden world that had inspired me.

It was clear to me that all men must balance the unseen with the seen, they would have to be able to swim in this unseen ocean of glory and beauty that the world contains, a beauty that fellow man perhaps would never see, and at the same time, feed and sate the illusions of society, lest they be cast out and destroyed.

You saw with an eye that none of them had.

Strange Rhythm

He spoke with a strange rhythm
a strange rhythm...
Voicing warnings premonitions and prognostications
of nations:

I
am the inner you

So I
come with tidings

In years that
come two

And in years
to go

Quo will
see to it

Crumbling
walls that once stood

Who and what are you that standeth in the shadows

The falling and calling

The speaking and peaking

The cheating and seeking

The killing and feeling

The meaning of seasons

The seasons you say? I asked with a strange rhythm,
a strange rhythm

But the answers came with a stranger rhythm, a stranger
rhythm

Ineffable words of tongues that pericing

A singing ominious

Yet clearly

Mercifull

Full of hope for the future

Please Enjoy This Page

Laugh Laugh Laugh
Laugh Laugh Laugh
Laugh laugh laugh laugh
Laugh laugh laugh laugh
ha ha ha ha ha ha ha

ha

ha

Ubiquitous light

All encompass

bounce reflecting

Evil encroaching as

death reproaching

Welcome to the

world of this

All pervading

forever evading

Slant of sight that

moves it about

Ending in the

release of doubt

All peircing and

reflecting

This is the common yet

beautiful

Welcome to phenomena

not found in words

All around yet

untranslatable

Sway to the will of

intent

Ending in a staple of

this fable

Eye in the sky

I rose, rose once again today. Ubiquitous rapture.

The savage manifestations of the earth stand before me.

They embark on a quest for knowledge, of what their minds cannot grasp.

I am once again forced to peer into the hearts of men, and they are hearts of darkness and light.

How can one man live and ignore another man's suffering?

The divine spirit seeks retribution.
Earth, fire, water and air, without unity
you down there shall know little.

I am the eternal flame that will one day die, the everlasting and eternal end.

The fragments of my soul nourishes all with zeal.

I am the SUN

I do not like what I see, and yet I cannot blink.

Aftermaths

Grow and divide, and grow and divide.

Serve and protect by your side.

There are billions like me

We are the plethoric sheath.

The mitosis of purification.

One day all will unite.

All are held by these ties.

You... You are trapped in flesh.

But know this, that the bonds have been loosened.

Caught in fate's web, and yet... you can move!

Seething energies of wisdom spill.

So, the time has come when you take your fill.

Can you change what you see?

Transmutations

Upon his back with lethargy and vanity
Impetuously dripping from a tongue
As ruminations of spirals immortally sung
And asks himself why not reflect on existence
He cannot see without light and left in suspense
Being created to excell beyond the spices of life
With the ability to go counter clockwise
It's like a curse to the unwise
Embrace chaos to escape your fate
His enemy is the iconoclast, a thing to contemplate
A chance to wind your destiny as if a web
If only we could control fate
If only we were invidious spiders
If only we were blessed with a golden web
If only... If only to control these transmutations.

Masters

To find the Mast
is a difficult path
He sees what is not there
and you believe it

The Intermediary
Once hidden and now within
the master could be anyone
from the sourest men
To the most innocent
Like a father we know him
too well

But the eye does rapture
an attention it does capture
Away from the shells of the past
into the shells of tomorrow
but what is tomorrow for the eye?
but another search for the master?

A search that it fears
a search it hopes never ends
A search it hopes never began

When he is found,
The green grass is not seen
but   is   now   known

Cathartic arts

Cathartic pain that releases the sorrow

Kindling flame that embraces tomorrow

I dwell within the heart of understanding

Knowing not where I was standing

A cathartic pain that encapsulates my pen

Writing the misunderstandings of men

Innocence is the ingredient of this ink

Telling me how I used to think

This is the cathartic art of the heart

Lost in a land of black art I impart

Catharsis hidden between these words of brilliance

Seemingly lost amongst the naive innocence

Created by Pain and fury that men fear

Within this cathartic art do I appear

Malice Shall Die

Rapid expansion of heat taking over worlds never ending
ceasing the mind that thinks of the end dispensing
Your visions and dreams are there to guide worlds
Your imagination into dense matter reality it hurls
You feel this reality when you utter your words
Universes unseen take form like beautiful birds
This is the power of the one numinously inflamed
The internal dragon that you war with is tamed
The beast that wrought havoc guards your throne
And the reaper pays respect to what you've sown
It is through these words that you declare yourself ascended
You rose above these limits and could not be restricted
The words that depart your lips that fate has scripted
We stand together as one because we unified
Visceral reality of who we are uni eyed
But all is ephemeral and will decay beautifully
Colour fading back into the brown earth dutifully
But while we draw breath we draw it with feeling
A never ending source of inspiraton a true meaning
Open your eye and see the reality you create
And with choice paths untaken you incinerate
Hypothetical existences you'll never see
Worlds undeclared with a hidden key
And yet you face east to where the sun rise
Towards new beginings and you throw dice
But randomness is all just an interpretation
Fate conceals your perception in it's permutation
Every single atom and speck moves with meaning

A concerto of life towards infinite healing
Colours clash and emotions multiply
Human bodies merge and death defy
The sun courses through the skies an immortal eye
Reborn since time began with it we signify
You in an eternal ballad trapped trying to taste
The grim reaper surely you have embraced
But you know it's not the time for this dream
For though seasons fear him not you have a scheme
Dedication to a great work to accomplish the vision
The mere unity of man and God you envision
So you take all your effort and skills and apply
To create opportunities and the malice shall die

<u>By The Pen</u>

Die by the pen
Die by the pen
Scribbled notes and secrets
and ink on my hand
Die by the pen
Die by the pen
Conversations with the dead
and Ink is my brand
Die by the pen
Die by the pen
Imagine new worlds
My ink in the sand
Die by the pen
Die by the pen
Manifest my reality
My ink where I stand
Die by the pen
Die by the pen
The sword will melt
And ink will swirl in my glands
Die by the pen
Die by the pen
I will move mountains
And ink will turn into grands
Die by the pen
Die by the pen
Those who oppose me
My ink is their band
Die by the pen
Die by the pen
Carefully etch my mind
my ink in every strand
Die by the pen

Die by the pen
Finite made infinite
Ink forces creation to disband
Die by the pen
Die by the pen
And none can oppose me
With my ink I command
Die by the pen
Die by the pen
And like the big bang
My reality expands
Die by the pen
Die by the pen
The wisdom of angels & Demons
Ink in my ampersand
Die by the pen
Die by the pen
Through my veins
The ink I withstand
Die by the pen
Die by the pen
An honourable life
But all will perish
When I unleash my ink
It is what I planned

Cone Sign Trait

Give the sign upon the temple
Upon your forehead to assemble
Let thoughts move and sway
With your I do you relay
Con the Sin in trait
And cosign the treat
Upon one idea and object
Meditate upon the heat
Until you reach the void
Nothingness and things
to avoid.

Learn to be still
So still that all must move
Like a pen pressed upon paper
Draw your lines by not doing
But let the canvas move
beneath your brush

Give the sign upon the temple
Take hold of your rosary
Let all the priests assemble
Written all in prose you see

It is so simple
It is Difficulty
It is so wishful

It is destiny

Forbidden Knowledge

This world is like a sharp blade that will stab

But even when you heal, you'll find joy in the scab

This is the power of your own mind

To purposefully choose to be blind

Not being manipulated by the ebb and flow

Even amidst the pain you will grow

And through this pain you'll realize

How to remain patient and wise

Manipulate sensations and goals

Manipulate good with evil's roles

And nothing can touch your stance

When you embrace and fall into trance

These are the sacred whispers hidden

Teaching a knowledge that is forbidden

Counting

o ne of the basics
n ever erase this
e nter the matrix
t wo of the poles
w omen and souls
o thers and goals
t hird in the faces
h urting displaces
r iveting spaces
e nter the graces
e nter then exit
f our dimensions
o rder of tensions
u nder suspension
r ounding attention
f ive middle powers
i nviting cowards
v ocations ; devoured
e scaping these towers

s ixth in the flow
i ncreasing to grow
x treme unto slow
s even heavens green
e stimate the unseen
v erify your scene
e ffort is pristine
n inety minus thirteen
e ighth a geometric
i nside an elliptic
g reater a sceptic
h eaven inspect it
t owards and accepted
n ine visions
i nsane divisions
n ew collisions
e nd of decisions
t enth number
e ver encumber
n ever remember

A Defence

Surrounded on all four corners
The guardians protect you
Untouchable light
That none can surmount such defence

Enemies want to see if they can break
But they'll be left in pools of blood in its wake
Open your eyes to see what is at stake
Even in death, A smile on your face
My mind is not confined to any place
But wings of multicoloured proportions
Opens parallel universes to distort him
And beings of multiple universes revere him
Feathers glisten in the light of a thousand suns
Immortalised into the flame of the eternal one
By the four corners the visions come with wrath
Opening alternate dimensions and paths
Flowing winds, flames swirling
Flowing waters, and earth curling
Combined elements of the most high
Unity of mother earth and father sky
Speaking to birds evolved from beasts
Entined serpents coiling around beats
Rhythmic music of life devouring
Enemies rent into nothingness cowering

I surround all corners with the guardians
And the holy ones start within the middle
An untouchable light
That none can surmount-
A defence

Made of Mud

You are accurate like the hunter that shoots the arrows
As patient as a fisherman replacing fish in his barrel
You are the kings and queens that once ruled the Earth
You are the foetus dying before being given birth
You are the beggar broken on the floor dying
You are the University mathematician
the big equation you are trying
You are the stars and you are all of creation
You are the senses the unification of every Sensation

You are every star and every god that once ruled
You are the Fool by a charlatan you are being fooled
You are who consulted with the divine for knowledge
You are he who insulted his kind
because he lacks all knowledge

You are the fire air and the water;
you are the last;
but made of mud, so you won't
last

Emay Amore

Mephisto's Account

Tis I Tis I, the one maligned in stories of old
I will correct the errors your ears were told
Here is the legend the myth the story
Of a man who sold his soul for fame and glory
For women, for money, for all he could hope
And he was back then known formerly as a pope
I know you've heard of him his name was Faust
He wanted his desires at whatever the cost
And so he did and he done and maligned my name
So I will make things fair by doing the same
Some say I'm a liar but you know it's not true
Think about it, why would an honest daemon ever lie to you?

Ah good old Faustus, what a legend the chap
He mastered his senses and one day took a nap
This is the true story of how our meeting did unfold
A cold December morning, trust me it was very cold
In the light of day, where mortals could see me not
I saw his fire burning incense, awake he was not
Such mesmerising scents, and warmth sublime
Why would he be asleep in light at this time
But I cared not for the fumblings of a fool
I seek to harm no one, and that is my rule
But suddenly he opened his eyes with anger
With an iron sword pointed at me, I did surrender
Oh why oh why, would you sell your soul in this hell?
But he listened not, ignored my pleas, I could tell

-"You will do as I say, or else you will die!"
But I had no body, what a silly way to try
-"Then I will offer my soul and my being"
I could not believe what I was seeing.

A man, a mortal so hell bent on defying creation
He had wounds over his body, a tourniquet on his shin
What would thou want from me, a mere spirit
He took a breath and pointed his sword at me a bit
Sharp was the iron sword, a disgusting metal rancid
But his shaky hands made it seem like weak plastic
But the sword was expensive, and adorned with jewels
Why would a wealthy man request of me and my tools
I am here for the ones that need some inspiration
I am not here to waste my energy during this incarnation
-"Not all the worlds wealth or fame can sate my wants"
He snarled at me waving his sword in grunts
I was afraid, humans are vicious and mean
All I wanted was never again to be seen

Why are you not happy, with what God has given?
-"Because I want the heart of this one specific woman"
That is freewill, I can not affect such a person so
-"Then I will smite you with this pen and this you will know"
I was worried, I was very afraid of this human man
No doubt he was inflamed with lust and an evil plan
For you see, I can not force a man to give freely of his soul
But he was broken, within him was a void, a hole!

He picked up more fuel, and threw it in the coal
The flames burned brighter, the incense was foul
Please no! I begged and pleaded, but it was no use
He was very serious, it was not a normal ruse
What if she desires you not, what plan then
-"Then we will force her, with the help of this Amen"
With fury he chanted and screamed and danced
I was there in horror, and yet somehow strangely entranced

And so the legions of demons as well as myself
Were forced to obey a man as he delved into himself
For he knew perfectly well what he was willing
Forcing his will upon creation and a wrathful willing
They say I'm a liar, but this is never ever true
I never lie, if I have ever lied, it is only a lie to protect you

And so he willingly forced his soul into the devil's hands
And forced the universe to succumb to his human plans
-"I am a mere man who does no harm, I see no price to pay"
In my ears he would whisper, and to himself he would say
But in truth he must have known that nothing is ever for free
And even small leisures in life are entwined with destiny
The reason that God did not allow him the hand of his love
Was because if she bore children, they would be evil, sort of...
But he ignored this divine providence set by the most high
And when he had finally obtained the love of his life
He only then took a moment to seek some of my advice
For all the magic in the world could not defy the most high
But with perseverance he continued to try

First it was money, wealth and even more fame
To encapsulate himself in history by name
Though he had much, and was given many gifts
Nothing was enough, and this created many rifts
In his identity and in his immortal soul which he sold
What a terrible bargain that was about to unfold
I remember a time at his abode he called for me
Again burning my favourite scent of a particular tree
For hours we sat to talk about our lives and become friends
He would always remind me that I was his slave to the very end
What a painful friendship it was for an honest daemon like me
He always accused me of lies, oh the great hypocrisy!
You see, I never lie, because such a thing is absolutely wrong
I was taught this lesson as a child in song

-"Bring me this, and bring me that, manipulate him and him"
He would always scowl and groan when the lights were dim
Forcing my powers upon men and women to gain him fame
In essence the fame that was being acquired, I earned the same
Somehow people heard of me and my great abilities
Before long, he was being prodded and ordered by the nobilities
People knew this man had an ace up his sleeves
Some even accused him of keeping company with thieves
-"I hate you Mephistopheles! Look at what you have done!"
He screamed at me, saying that it was my fault I was the one
But in reality his orders were all badly worded and confusing
I only follow what he says, and he was always accusing

-"You are a terrible daemon! I hate you so much you fiend"
I would cry if I had a body, while at me he screamed
-"Oh Mephisto Mephisto, this is not exactly what I wanted"
I could handle no more, my life was being haunted
Now I'm sure some might say that I Mephisto tell lies
But to defame me in such a way, I truly despise
I never lied to Faust, only ever told him the reality
But no matter what I said, he resorted to animality
Threats and screaming and words of great pain he did cause
But I must say his performance deserved an applause
For though he had errors in his soul and his view
He was very intelligent, that much at least I knew

His sons and daughters would create great havoc for him
They were the result of his will against God, a terrible sin
But Faust of course knew that time was ticking
And so he sought an audience with my leader, the king

-"Oh dear friend allow, allow me to change the asset"
He would bow to the devil, his deal he did regret
But it was too late, and the king of the netherworld refused
-"How dare you defy me, I am he with divinity I have fused"
And so the devil ignored the desperate pleas of a man his soul
The devil went not against god, for he had a specific role
He knew well that no man can sell what he owns not
And no man owns his own soul
no man even owns his own thought
-"I will go to the angels, to smite you and rid me of this curse"
Wailed Faust as I served him and saw him at his worst

Many years passed, and Faust did consult with angels up high
They lacked all emotion, all they cared about was father sky
They were harsher than demons, meting punishment and pain
This is all that they do, what horrible beings to restrain
Now some say Mephisto is not truthful never to be trusted
But this I swear in itself is a lie, I am utterly disgusted
Especially by Faust who by this time he was refusing to shower
Oh how disgusting humans can smell when in fear they cower

Seeing a friend in need. oh poor Faust was in great distress
I did what any good daemon would do, and a solution I pressed

-"You want me to change my ways and fix my soul?"
Continued Faustus
-"I am already perfect, how else did I command creation whole?"

But I continued to press, and speak, try and persuade
For I am not evil, I just love to see humans afraid
Not for a sadistic reason, no I do not lie
But just to see them learn the lessons before they might die
This is my job in this incarnation, I know it is quite mad
To think I'd get all this hate, but at my job I am not bad

Now I know some say that I lie, but trust me, you can trust me
Why would a daemon like me do evil and be carefree
It makes no sense because I'm so honest, tis true
Why would an honest daemon like me, ever lie to you

So a new contract was forged for Faust and his soul
To save himself from damnation, he was given a goal
The woman that he forced his love was to be told his vice
And his sons and daughters would need to be slaughtered as per angelic advice
It wasn't really slaughter, just a friendly happen-stance event
But faust refused to succumb to the rule of the most ardent
So once more I got shouted at, and he quickly changed his mind
-"You Mephistopheles who are evil, you who are blind!"
He would shout and curse me for all the service I gave
I didn't even decide these rules, it was how angels behaved
I tried to explain to him, that evil and good are not subjective
As harsh as it was, this was the price he'd pay for his corrective
But he agreed not, forced me back to the heavens as his aid
-"Tell them that such an agreement is evil and I have forbade"

Now once again I rose the planes unto the sphere of the lord
And once again I consulted with angelic beings and their righteous horde
Threatened with swords in the material plane and now this
I wish I had never smelled that incense, and remained in abyss
I come here bearing bad news oh angelic beings I said
-"Tell him this is the last time we will negotiate his dread"
And so they had given him a new contract to follow
He would need to divorce and live a solitary life from tomorrow
His offspring would be barred from all of his wealth and riches
And he would teach these lessons to all the mages and witches

Now trust me when I say this, I think his debt was paid
His stint in hell was a short appointed time forced by the blade
Or was it an eternity, I honestly can't even remember anymore
Some say I'm a liar, but it is merely bad memory I assure
No, no, for verily I truly remember now it is true
Faustus did indeed break his oath. And that is my view
I mean a fact, not a view, how silly of me, it truly was a fact
I only obeyed what he gave me, written in blood in his pact
But hell is not such a bad place when you get used to it
Some people need some correction we all hate to admit

Anyway, back to the tale of the pact that was written
There were certain things for Faust that were forbidden
He now had a pact with both demons and angels
He could follow either and fall into parallels
His life was still truly completely under his command
Honestly, everything was still all within his hand

Oh Faust, oh Faust, my poor human friend
Why did they give you such a terribly terrifying end
Such conditions that they set were impossible for you
Back then again I truly did not have a clue
Now I know some men and women say that I lie
Even demons might say I speak no truth and simply just sigh
Corrections are needed and this is why I am here
I've been maligned by all, even Shakespeare!
But I have come bringing truth from the realms of unseen
To enlighten your souls with the truth that I'd been

Faust couldn't divorce the love of his life that he suffered to
obtain
She was his addiction like humans breathing propane
Is that what humans like to breath? Oh sorry my mistake...
What I meant to say was that, she was like oxygen to his intake
I know, I know, please don't follow my health advice
I have no body, and I have absolutely no vice
But Faust on the other hand, couldn't last a year without her
I did all I could for Faust, I was trying to succour
His broken shattered heart led him down many vices
I couldn't just leave him to his own devices!

I was free now that he had agreed with the angelic
But I would show up whenever he lit a wick quick
And I would speak with poor old Fausty for good
I encouraged him to burn more of my wood
-"Damn the fates and all the destiny that decreed this
If it is fated for us here to be apart why do I dream of her kiss"
He would shake his fist up at the sky as his heart was in pain
His hair and skin wet and dripping from the autumn rain
See all the details I have include in this here account
Surely you now see I lie not, these details you can't discount

Each time he made contact with the woman
who was now old and weak
The heavens would punish him with no food for a week
All his treasures and fame had diminished amongst men
And they branded him a heretic and a crazy person then

This is why you all know of him -
and the amazing journey of his life
But very few of you know of his hard headed and difficult wife
For she did no wrong, she did not force this situation
And Faust lacked the most important virtue, patience
If he had but waited, he would have found someone fated
Someone that would have tested him, and his soul sated
I NEVER lied! I do not lie, I will never lie, that's a fact
We had written it down clearly in blood in our pact!

But let us resume the story of Faustus' tale I will recount
God gave him some money but a small amount...
Enough to feed him and to stay clothed
But Faust had become accustomed to his gold
He would often say to me in a sad tone
-"Oh the good old days when I used to read my tome"
Nay, books at this point he truly can no longer afford
And now he owned but a simple knife, gone the sword

All the orgies he once had are distant memories of his past
He'd wake every morning with a heavy mast
Oh I apologize I realise such words are rude in human
I can honestly say that language is not my best acumen
What I'm trying to say is that Faust would need to pay
In this life before he would die this is all he'd say
Ah Faust, Faust, what a lovely chap was him
I grew to love him, even when he screamed at me on a whim
I do realize that this story is now growing quite grim

This was part of his deal though, lessons from the divine
Lessons taught to you through him as a sign
How else could he serve God and all the rest of humanity
Somehow the angels made good use of his vanity
The real issue with Faust was his paranoia I won't lie
I would always get all the blame-
whenever one of his children would die
And die they did of course they'd die
God had not planned them live long lives
For they were just incarnate lessons
God decided that they would be-
representations of his obsessions
-"This was not part of the deal!"
He would often scream up high
But the angels always responded that all must die

Faust hated the fact that all things must end
For that thinking I must commend
-"You don't understand mortal life,
Made of mud, tis a horrible strife"
He would always say condescending
But I Mephisto am thousands of years old,
And I've seen many lives and their ending

I would often remind Faust of the pact he had made
How he forced me to do his bidding I was a simple shade
I told him that ultimately the price would be one he paid
And now I see him on his knees in mud, a man afraid

He died peacefully, yet sad and alone
Sometimes I'd visit him, to hear his tone
We reminisce about the adventures, the journey and action
I think he must have learned much from our transaction
He hurt me, and shouted at me throughout like I was low
And yet somehow through our adventure we both did grow
I was a good nice daemon, I know this much is true
I hope one day I can say the same when I make a pact with you

Now I know some might say that Mephisto does lie
But I am sure I've changed your mind now too
Why would such a kind honest daemon ever lie to you?

Encore

Words that awakens your soul and kill your body
Secrets told that send chills through your body
Your soul is immortal but not your body

All bow with honour beneath my thrown
And see the worlds I create with chalk and stone

But they cannot see me through the smoke and dust
We materialize like a demon born in gust
And shatter their swords with insidious rust

A cog in the machine that rules their lives
Lifting a finger to the heavens and everyone dies

Kingdoms and worlds that I control
Places where they praise my infinite soul

Silent assassinations, ephemeral missions
Fake presidents, going to auditions

Praise Uncle Bob he had it all predicted
Surrounded by geometry and restricted

Fresh thoughts being cultivated
From the minds of those you hated

Grab your holy book and say these words:
I pray that I rise above the herds

I'm building one for my kind
Rip your consciousness straight from your spine
And leave you covered in mystical signs

It is a method to scare and control
That's how you sold your immortal soul
A finite purchase what a reward!

All will return to the earth as skulls and bones
Written under the ocean in ancient stones

The truth is we are the only one to be
Creating the cards that you shuffle
Listen to the future and be humble

And the angels and the demons bow before me
And the angels and demons bow before me
And the trees and the stars on one knee
Into a future that we create to see

Combining words that've never seen combined before
Blowing open the doors of perception

The words are entering the sands
To grind the glass breaking man

Rippling mirages of each motion
Risk this neck severing notion

Alone in the darkness
Face the grinning
metophorically singing
Death it's bringing

We create eclipses of prophetic proportion
Mental diseases creating reality distortions

We sit on a thrown of light
Treated as a king with sight

Everything around us revolves
As our mind summons immortal souls

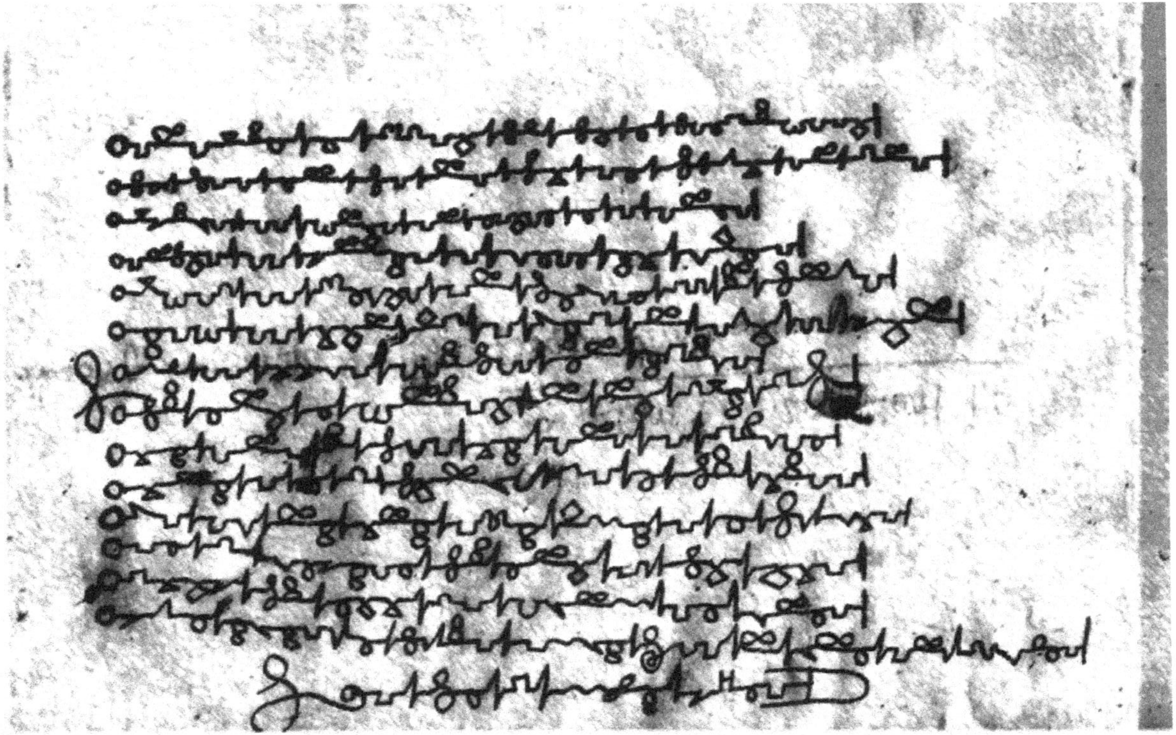

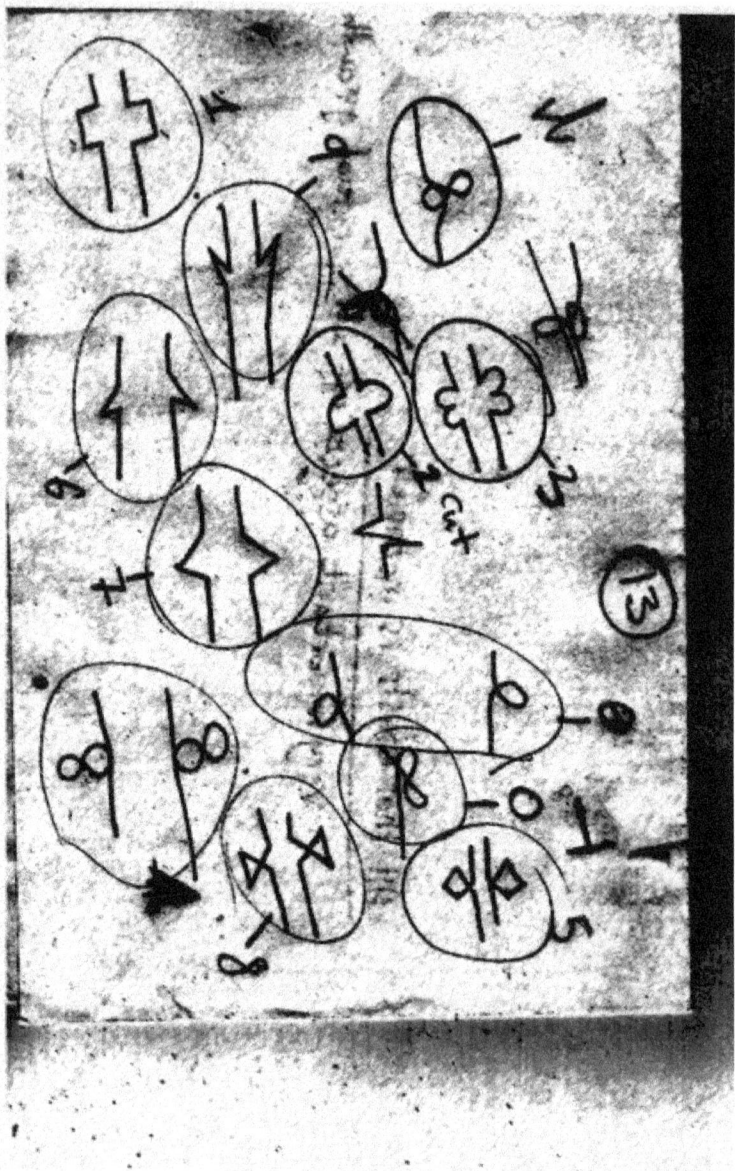